MW00783826

Mosaic Birds & Butterflies

Original step-by-step design made from ceramic and glass

Sigalit Eshet

Copyright © Sigalit Eshet

All rights reserved.

First Print Edition: 2024

Photographs by Efrat Tenenbaum and Sigalit Eshet

Translation: Michaeli Translations

ISBN: 978-965-93065-2-7

www.sigalit.art

All rights reserved. No part of this book, text, photographs or illustrations may be reproduced or transmitted in any form or by any means whether electronic, optical or mechanical (including photocopy, recording, Intermesh and e-mail). Commercial use of any kind of the content of this book is strictly prohibited without an authorization detailed in writing by the author.

Readers are permitted to reproduce any of the items/patterns in this book for their personal use. Any use of the items/patterns for commercial purpose is not permitted without a prior permission of the Author.

Thank you for respecting the hard work of this author.

Disclaimer

All do-it-yourself activities involve risk, and your safety is your own responsibility, including proper use of equipment and safety gear, and determining whether you have adequate skill and experience.

Some of the resources used for these projects are dangerous unless used properly and with adequate pre-cautions, including safety gear.

Some illustrative photos do not depict safety precautions or equipment, in order to show the project step more clearly.

Some projects are user-submitted, and appearance of a project in this format does not indicate it has been checked for safety or functionality. Use of the instructions and suggestions is at your own risk.

I disclaim all responsibility for any resulting damage, injury, or expense. It is your responsibility to make sure that your activities comply with all applicable laws.

Contents

Introduction

The art of mosaic is an ancient one. It started many years ago with natural stone, which was manually cut into little pieces and put together to make an image. We can still find mosaic floors and walls in different places around the world, amazed by their richness and colorfulness, or the way they were preserved.

There's a wide range of materials nowadays, new shapes are added as time goes by, and there's more variety – something that makes us, mosaic creators, very happy. The art of mosaic allows anyone to create in whatever way they choose: whether cutting ceramics, gluing on ready-made pieces, recycling or using cut-up cups and plates, working with glass, or combining various materials in one piece and practically painting with them.

My name is Sigalit, I'm a long-time mosaic artist who creates, teaches and spreads the art of mosaic throughout the world via books and workshops that make it accessible for anyone who wishes to make mosaics and doesn't know where to start.

As someone who's been a mosaic artist for many years, I admit I had fallen in love with it because of its colorfulness, range of materials, and various techniques; as well as the possibility to innovate, invent, and work both creatively and technically. As a former puzzle enthusiast, I find mosaic answers that same need, providing countless hours of relaxation, creativity, and the ability to give wings to your imagination.

The saying, "From all who taught me have I gained understanding" is very true in my case. I am glad to say that I've learned from each project and every student of mine, and had a great time adopting all the little "tips" that help in and develop the process of mosaic making. And this, all while creating new designs which I gladly share with my readers and students. I am excited each time as I see my designed mosaics online, inspiring students from all over the world!

A little bit about me: I live in a small village, surrounded by trees and lawns. I wake up to the sound of chirping birds most of the year, and so I've noticed that I've created a lot of them. This is why I decided to dedicate this book to the beloved birds, and the butterflies that accompany them, and produce a unique mosaic book on this topic.

In the book, you can find many examples for mosaic work on birds and butterflies, including waterbirds and other kinds: owls, various types of butterflies, 3D works, use of glass and ceramics, a combination of materials, pictures for the house, or mosaic on walls. The projects are followed by images that depict how to create them step-by-step, along with printable patterns (you should download the file at the end of the book). You can always change the colors, or replace materials, as you prefer or according to the existing materials you have at your disposal, and of course, go on creating as you get inspired by your surroundings.

This is the tenth mosaic book in the series, and I hope you'll enjoy it as much as the ones before, and that it gives you ideas for creating your next mosaic works.

I guarantee you a fun and colorful experience!

Sigalit

Mosaic Cutting Tools

There are various tools used in mosaic work. You should first have the basic ones.

I should start by mentioning that there is a tool designated for each material you use. Using the right tool can make the work easier, and make the cutting of the pieces more precise. There are various cutters for cutting tiles, at different prices. The difference between them is mainly the sturdiness of the tool and its cutting technique. Also notice the handles – they should be comfortable.

Since this book offers using various materials, I recommend that you have at least one of each of the tools, especially a glass and ceramics cutting tool. You can obviously make the suggested patterns from any material you choose.

Later on, you could find detailed instructions on how to work with each tool. Below are detailed instructions on working with each instrument.

Ceramic Cutting

Mosaic Tile Cutter (1) – For cutting and grinding ceramic tiles. You can get these in hardware stores.

Compound Tile Nipper (2) – For cutting and grinding ceramic tiles. This tool has twice the power of a conventional cutter. You can find it online or in specialized stores. I love using this tool, as it's strong and easy to cut with.

Combined Tile Cutting Clamp (3) – A technique taken from glass sheet cutting. Using the clamp, you first make notches in the tile and then cut it. A simple replacement to a cutting machine or curved cuts.

Parrot Beak Nipper (4) – Intended for making dents in tiles, when you want to make curved and dented shapes, such as hearts.

Ceramic Cutting Machine – For advanced cutters. Used to cut ceramic into straight and accurate tiles. I did not use this cutting machine for any projects in this book.

Hammer – For cutting thick ceramic, or when you want to cut random shapes. Please note that when you cut ceramic with a hammer, you should wrap the ceramic with an old towel and place it on top of a thick wood or metal surface.

Glass Cutting Tools

Wheeled Glass Nipper – For cutting glass and plates.

For cutting any kind of glass – surfaces or squares – as well as cutting plates and cups. Can be found in stores that sell glass cutting equipment.

If you wish to integrate glass from a large panel into the mosaic, you'll need several other tools used for cutting glass (also used for making stained glass). I like using these panels for their shine and pleasing appearance, and since they come in a wide variety of colors. There are also places that sell pre-cut glass strips of glass, which can sometimes make it easier to cut.

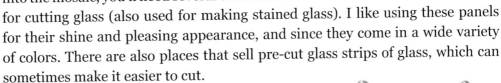

Glass Cutter – For cutting straight lines or specific shapes. There are several kinds of cutters. The difference is in shape and price. I recommend that you try out and decide which cutter works best for you. All cutters have a small wheel at the top, and the difference is mainly in the grip angle.

Pliers

Breaking glass plier/Running plier – For Breaking glass after marking it with the glass cutter.

Grozer pliers - For breaking glass along score lines that can't be handled comfortably by hand. The cutter has two sides, one straight and the one curved.

Mosaic Equipment and Preparation Tools

The additional mosaic making tools are not expensive and can easily be attained:

Pencil – For drawing the desired pattern on the substrate material.

Ruler – For marking straight lines.

T-Ruler – For guiding the glass cut into straight lines.

Tweezers – For placing small pieces.

Glass Paint Marker – For marking shapes on the glass. It's better to have one black and one white or gold, for dark glass panels.

Latex Gloves – For protecting your hands against scratches and dirt.

Rubber Gloves – Put these on before you start working with grout.

Plastic Containers – For glue, water, cut glass or beads and mixing colors.

Small Brush – For cleaning the surface from dust and small particles.

Thin Flat Screwdriver – For cleaning tile adhesive residue.

Paintbrush – For adhesive application.

Wooden Mixing Sticks – For mixing grout and applying tile adhesive.

Carbon Paper – To copy your design from paper onto your substrate material.

Spatula – For applying tile adhesive. This tool is usually used by painters but is very efficient in applying tile adhesive.

Safety Equipment

Safety goggles – For protecting your eyes against ceramic fragments. Use it when cutting ceramic.

Dust mask – Use this when preparing the grout.

Safety Instructions

Safety is imperative when making mosaic. Glass and cut ceramic have sharp edges and can shoot out toward you, so use caution.

1. Always wear closed shoes. Don't walk barefoot on the floor where you are working. Small fragments can be difficult to spot and remove.
2. Wear safety goggles and gloves when cutting glass plates.
3. Use a small brush to clean the working surface. Don't clean the small fragments with your bare hands!
4. Vacuum the floor after finishing – it's better than just sweeping dust around.
5. Keep young children and pets away.
6. Keep some adhesive bandages at hand.

Materials

The list of materials that can be used for mosaic works can be very long, which is what I like so much about it – you can, and should combine different types of materials, depending on the type of work you're choosing to do, of course. Some materials are more gentle and only fit works that will stay indoors, while others will last outdoors for many years. Some materials have to be cut, while others come ready-made, and all you have to do is style and glue them on.

In this book, you'll find diversified works that can be made by using various material combinations. I suggest experimenting and choosing the materials with which you'd like to work. In works that fit outdoors, please avoid using plastic pieces that might fade in the sun or peel off. Additionally, please note what kind of treatment the material needs and what is the best glue for the job. For instance, when working with natural stone, you should apply a sealer at the end, so as to accentuate the stone's natural colors. Other materials don't react well when applied with grout, which is why you should avoid it.

The following list contains the best materials for your mosaic works, but you can obviously try and combine any materials you see fit, or anything special you might find:

Colorful Ceramic Tiles – Can be found in a variety of shapes and sizes.

Glass Tiles – These come in uniform size squares and in many colors. They have one smooth, flat side (which should face up), and a rough side (to which glue is applied).

Stained Glass – Can be found in many colors and textures. You can cut it with a nipper or a glass cutter.

Ceramic Square Tiles – These are available in many colors, textures, and shapes. They come mostly on a square mesh.

Vitreous Glass Mosaic Tiles – Ready-made square glass tiles in a variety of sizes and colors. The glass can be glossy or grainy, clear or opaque, uniform or blended. Tile sizes start at $1 \text{ cm}^2/0.15\text{in}^2$, and you can buy them by sheets of sticker tiles or by weight.

China and Crockery – Using the proper safety precautions, these can be broken or used to cut your own tiles. Plates often have that unique texture that you can't find in tiles.

Found Objects – These include seashells, glass beads, buttons, glass nuggets, necklaces, brooches, etc. Use it to decorate and enrich your work.

Mirrors – These can add a beautiful reflective touch to any mosaic piece.

Polymer clay – Use polymer clay, like Fimo™, to decorate your mosaic work.

Beads – I like incorporating different types of beads into mosaics: glass or plastic, round or square, tiny or large. Each necklace that falls out of my favor ends up in my bead box, and quickly finds its way into a mosaic piece.

Smalti – Colored glass chunks with very vivid colors. We'll leave the smalti for more advanced installments; the book will not cover this material.

Adhesives

Remember that it is essential to correctly use adhesives! You should always read the manufacturer's instructions. I recommend that you use the adhesive that is most comfortable for you.

It is very important to match the adhesive to the piece's base material. For instance, when you glue on a wooden surface, only use white glue. This glue suits mosaic works that will not come in contact with water, moisture, or direct sunlight; meaning, pieces that will be stored in a safe place or will be used as a temporary adhesive for gluing on meshes.

In cases that the piece's base is metal, concrete or ceramics; or in cases that we have chosen to create a mosaic that will remain outdoors, you should use tile adhesive – this way, the piece will have no problem remaining outside, in any weather.

There are many types of adhesives. I will detail the ones we shall use in this book:

Tile Glue – Used to glue ceramic tiles on metal, clay, or any other surface intended for outdoors, and are exposed to the elements. This glue comes in powder form that needs to be mixed with water (make as much as you need each time) or in a ready-made box (for instance, Sheramik). Once it settles, the glue becomes stone hard, that is why you have to work with a small batch every time.

Glass Glue – For sticking tiles onto a glass substrate (like E6000).

Silicone Glue – Arrives in a tube and is for gluing relatively small surfaces. Useful for gluing wall tiles when you are looking for a quick and strong gluing. You should choose a gluing adhesive and not a sealing one (like Super 7).

Carpenter's Glue – Used as a temporary adhesive for gluing on a mesh, before gluing the work onto the surface using tile adhesive.

White Glue – Used to glue mosaic on wood surface.

Tips for Using Adhesives

Each adhesive comes with its own instructions. However, there are a few use options, and you can choose the best one for you each time, according to the following specifications:

Tile glue:

1. When creating the mosaic, you should transfer a little at a time to a smaller container, and add more each time you run out, since this glue dries out quickly.

2. It's recommended to first find the exact place in which the chosen stone would be placed, and only then apply glue on the other side of it and glue it in place. This is how you reach maximal accuracy and keep the spaces between the stones to a minimum.

3. When working on a large surface or a straight line, you can apply glue on the surface and place the stones, one after the other.

4. Using a spatula – you can apply the glue using a wooden stick, but it's better to use a spatula (palette knife) with a narrow head.

5. Piping bag – one of the nice tricks is using a piping bag to apply the glue, in order to keep the work tidy. Try it and you won't look back...
   - Take a transparent, baking piping bag.
   - Fold the rims and fill it with tile glue.
   - Straighten the rims of the bag and close with a clip.
   - Cut the tip of the bag and leave a small hole.
   - "Pipe" the glue when you need it.
   - Once finished, you can keep the bag in a closed box. Even if the tip of the bag dries out, the glue inside stays fresh and you can take off the dry part before using it again.

White glue:

1. When making the mosaic, you should put a bit of glue in a small container, so it doesn't dry out.

2. This glue is usually more convenient when using a paint brush.

3. Another option: put some glue in a container with a thin tip, and apply directly from the bottle.

4. If you want to be precise, you should first find the right place for the stone and only then apply the glue on the back side of it, and glue it in place.

5. When working on a large surface or a straight line, you can apply the glue on the surface and place the stones on it, one after the other.

Grout

Grout is a colorful powder mixed with water and used to fill in the gaps between the tiles – usually floor and wall tiles. In mosaic work, grout is used as a finisher, to fill the gaps between the cut tiles. In addition, it reinforces the work and brings all the pieces together for one complete work. The grout also levels the height differences between the cut tiles and smoothens the mosaic. Later on, we will see several situations in which the grout can be expanded in its usage as a finisher.

The grout comes in different colors that are matched to the project. White grout can be diversified using acrylic paint or color pigments, as long as the final work is not being exposed to sun or water. It is important to make the mixture itself according to the manufacturer's instructions.

Working with grout might get messy, so it is important to wear the right clothes, cover the surface with a newspaper and put on gloves. You should set aside time in your day to apply the grout since you cannot stop in the middle – the mixture will harden and will be very hard to clean.

Before applying the grout, make sure the following is ready:

A Plastic Container – For making the grout.

Wooden Stirring Sticks – For mixing the grout.

Latex Gloves – For protecting your hands.

A Small Plastic Wiper or Spatula (a silicone spatula for cream) – For picking up and applying the grout on even surfaces.

Sponge or Cotton Rags – For grout cleaning.

Old Newspapers – For placing under your work to maintain a clean surface.

Water – For preparing grout and cleaning.

Choosing the Right Color Grout

The color of grout you select will significantly influence the final look. In fact, if you create the exact same piece twice, but with different grout finishes, the mosaic will look utterly different.

When choosing the grout color, ask yourselves what you want to emphasize – the shape or the background? Perhaps the harmony of the mosaic?

A few tips to help you choose the most appropriate color:

1. If your mosaic has a main subject and a background, make sure the background blends in and does not contest the subject. Figure out which color can highlight the main image, should it be light or dark, and what will its effect on the subject be.

2. If you're not sure about the right color of grout – gray seems to always get the job done. It's a neutral color suitable for most pieces. Remember that the final work will have a lighter shade than when it's wet during the processing.

3. Pieces with colored glass should be complemented with dark grout, as it emphasizes and intensifies the glass colors.

4. Sometimes it's best to treat grout as an additional color in the work, which gives it more depth. Here, you should use colored grout that will blend in with the mosaic without taking over.

5. Try to avoid using white grout – it highlights blemishes in the work. Use it when you wish to accentuate a white look or when the mosaic is glued tightly on a white background.

6. You can pour a little grout powder into the crack between the tesserae in one of the piece's corners to test and see which color you get.

7. Sometimes, when working with tile glue, it is hard to clean up after and parts of the adhesive may fill up the gaps between the tiles. In this case, grout in the same color as the adhesive (usually cream) would fit.

Project: Black Bird on a Feathers Background

In this image, for example, I wanted to incorporate both a bird and feathers. The inspiration for this image came from the black birds with the yellow beaks (mynas) that I see in my garden every day.

In some works, we separate the background from the object, but in this case, it was important for me to show that both the object and the background were equally present. So, I laid colorful feathers around the bird, creating harmony and a colorful rainbow.

Materials:

- A fiberglass mesh cut into a rectangle at your desired size
- A nylon sheet, slightly larger than the mesh
- Ceramics in shades of black, red, orange, yellow, light green, dark green, blue. Purple, light blue, and white
- Little gray squares
- A yellow circle for the eye
- A ceramic cutting nipper
- Paint brush
- Tweezers
- White glue or carpenter glue
- Scissors
- Little saucer for glue
- Tile glue
- A little spackle to apply the glue
- A small screwdriver or toothpick to clean the excess glue
- Dark-gray grout
- Grout equipment: bowl, water, mixing stick, spatula, rags, paper, and gloves.

Pattern for the bird:
Copy and enlarge according to the desire size.

1 Print out the bird pattern and mark the page with the desired feathers order. Cut out a nylon mesh to fit. Use a stapler to connect the three pieces in the following order: bird image, a nylon sheet over it, followed by the mesh. In a small container prepare carpenter glue and a paint brush (see tips on how to work with carpenter glue on page 19).

2 Cut narrow strips of black ceramics (see explanation on page 22) and glue them on the mesh tightly, along the width of the wing. It's important to maintain the same gluing direction. In order to emphasize the wing and separate it from the bird's body, glue a line of yellow ceramic squares at its edge. Add the yellow eye, and a beak by using a red triangle.

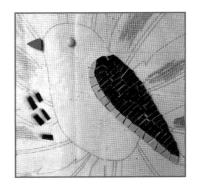

3 Glue the same black strips on the bird's body, this time in a different direction – vertically, to separate it from the wing.

4 Cut gray squares in two and glue thin contours to create the center of the feathers. If you are using glass squares, you should use a glass nipper to cut them.

5 Cutting the feathers: in order to get the shape of the feathers, you should first cut the ceramics into long strips. Each strip is then cut diagonally with the nipper to get a contoured cut at the end that would fit the shape of the feathers.

6 In order to make things easier, you should cut the feather pieces in advance. You can use a separated plate to keep the colors apart.

7 Bird's tail: glue black strips along the tail to create a continuity to the bird's body. Also, cut out triangles to help give the tail its feathery look, like it shows in the picture.

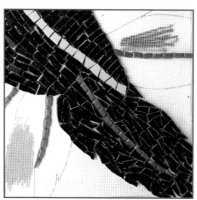

8 All the feathers are glued together in the same way and style. Start from the green feathers. Glue green pieces on both sides of the gray strip, while keeping the diagonal feather direction.

9 Glue the rest of the feathers in the same way, one after the other. It's important to maintain the picture frame straight.

10 Cut white ceramics into little pieces and complete the background.

11 Wait a few days for it to dry, separate the mesh from the nylon and cut it as close as possible to the mosaic.

12 Put on gloves. Use a spackle to apply tile glue on the back side of the work. How much glue? Depends on how straight the wall is on which you're about to glue the work.

13 Put the bird picture up against the wall and press tightly. You can gently pound it with your hands or a wooden hammer, to completely stick the pieces. Take out the residue glue sticking out by using a thin screwdriver, before it all dries up.

14 Wait for it to dry for at least 24 hours. Make dark-gray grout and apply it, using a plastic spatula, directly onto the wall. Clean and shine it using a sponge or wet rags (see detailed explanations on page 27).

TIP: Working with carpenter glue

There are two ways to work with this glue: one, apply it directly onto the mesh, and the other, apply it on the designated part. When it comes to small parts, such as an eye or a beak, it's better to apply the glue on the part itself. When applying a colorful strip or a surface, you should apply it directly onto the mesh. Notice, apply a small surface at a time, since the glue dries up quickly.

Using the Nipper to Cut Various Random Glass Shapes

Before cutting, put on safety goggles to protect your eyes from small fragments.

Hold the glass nipper with your dominant hand by its bottom element. Use your other hand to hold the glass. Place the glass between the wheels and cut away. The shape you'll get depends on the angle and manner in which you hold the glass. Over time, you'll learn to control the nipper grip and succeed in creating whatever shape you like.

To cut (relatively) straight lines, it's important to hold the nipper at a straight angle to the glass.

To cut a triangle shape, hold the nipper in an angle and cut to the desired shape.

Tip: When cutting glass, small pieces might ricochet. It is recommended to cut it into a wide and tall bowl (or even a plastic box). You should use gloves while cutting as to avoid any cuts and bruises.

Using the Mosaic Cutter

Before cutting, wear safety goggles to protect your eyes from small fragments.

1 Hold the bottom of the cutter with your dominant hand, with the curved side facing toward the ceramic. Hold the ceramic tile in your other hand, and in your dominant hand, hold the bottom of the cutter handle.

2 Hold the ceramic tile with the cutter in a straight or diagonal orientation for the type of crop you want, and clip!

3 If you want to cut small pieces or shape the tile, hold the tile by the widest part of the cutter and clip.

Cutting Ceramic Strips:

The ceramic tile strips can be cut in two ways:

1. Using a cutting machine – set the desired strip width and cut all tiles to the same width strips.
2. Use a combined nipper.

Cutting stripes with combined pliers

This device combines two devices used to cut glass. A knife that scratches the tile, and pliers that break in half. If you're experienced in cutting glass, you already know the technique.

1 Place the wheeled nipper at the bottom of the tile and groove it from bottom to top. It's recommended to press the nipper and stabilize the hand to get a straight groove.

2 Place the tile between the two nipper parts, exactly at the center of the groove, and click.

3 The tile will break in half along the entire groove.

4 Use a ceramic nipper to cut out little triangles. It's recommended to make a lot of triangles ahead of time.

Project: Bird on a Pot Lid

One of the things I love most about making mosaics is recycling. In fact, every mosaic work is a connection and combination between recycled materials that create something new. You can and should use dishes that are no longer in use as a basis for your mosaic, and create wonderful works.

This bird was created on the lid of a metal pot, which is a great basis for mosaic since it can endure outdoors in any weather, and doesn't need an additional hanger; only remove the handle and you get a round surface that's simply waiting to be refreshed.

You can use a variety of materials and look at the lid as a picture, meaning that you can mix materials in different sizes and thickness. In this case, I used ready-made glass squares, some are intact, and others were cut, even the glass plates from which I had cut the required shapes. Additionally, I chose a unique color scale.

Materials:

- A metal pot lid
- 1 cm glass squares in various colors: blue, light blue, red, orange, black, brown, cream
- 0.5 cm black glass squares
- White-pink glass for the background
- An eye-shaped bead
- Red and blue glass squares or glass plates
- Gray glass for the tail
- Wheeled nipper
- Tile glue
- Toothpick or a narrow screwdriver
- A glue container
- A wooden stick or spatula
- Cream-colored grout
- Grout equipment: Bowl, water, mixing stick, spatula, rags, newspaper, and gloves.

1 Take off the lid's handle (usually screwed on).

2 Print out the pattern at the desired size and trace the bird onto the lid. Since you cannot use a tracing paper, you can use the following methods:

- Cut out the circle with the drawing of the bird.
- Flip the paper with the printed-out pattern to the other side.
- Paint the outline of the painting using a strong oil pastel color. This will be used as a substitute for the tracing paper.
- Flip the paper over and position it in place on the metal lid. It's recommended to tape the edges of the paper, so it doesn't move.
- Using a pencil, press down and trace all the outlines to trace the pattern to the surface.

3 Using a permanent marker, trace the outlines of the pattern on the lid.

4 The tail: trace the pattern onto a gray glass and cut each shape with the glass cutting knife (see explanation on cutting shapes from glass on page 37).

5 Glue the tail parts in place using tile glue and clean the rest of the glue around them by using a toothpick or narrow screwdriver.

6 The wing: using the wheeled nipper, cut up blue or other varied glass into different sized pieces and glue them closely together (see explanation on cutting with a wheeled nipper later on).

7 Cut-up glass squares into thin strips using a wheeled nipper, in order to create the bird's body.

8 Glue the cut-up strips one to the other in a certain order, to create a flowing pattern.

9 The legs of the bird are made out of little orange squares cut in two. Cut a glass triangle for the beak.

10 Glue on a frame made out of small, black squares.

11 For the background: cut-up white-pink glass into random shapes and fill in the whole background, close together. (see explanation on cutting glass on page 21).

12 Set the order of colors for the background and glue one row after the other, as closely as possible. You can combine different shapes, depending on the size of the lid. You should cut the squares in two in the bottom part of the lid; it will make it easier to glue them.

Pattern for the bird:
Copy and enlarge according to the desire size.

13 Prepare cream-colored grout according to the manufacturing instructions. Apply it and clean until the glass is shiny. The picture is ready! Hang on a strong nail or screw wherever you want, indoors or outdoors.

Applying a grout, step by step:

1 Put on a dust mask to protect your face, and wear gloves.

2 Cover the work surface with old newspapers.

3 Add a few teaspoons of the desired colored grout (in this case, cream) into a plastic bowl or a disposable container.

4 Pour a bit of water into the bowl. Mix with a wooden stick until the consistency is cream-like. Notice the manufacturer's instructions to achieve best results.

5 Start the application process: pour a bit of the grout onto the work. Using a plastic spatula, spread the grout until it fills up all the grooves and holes. Make sure to fill grout also on the sides.

6 Once everything is covered with grout, use the side of the spatula in order to scrape off and remove any excess grout.

7 After a few minutes, once the grout starts to set, start cleaning: Dampen the piece using a clean cotton rag or a sponge. Use a wet (squeezed) and dry rag several times until the piece is clean. Make sure to change the water every once in a while.

8 If you find any "holes" after cleaning, fill them up with grout, wait until it dries out, and clean until you get a smooth and clean mosaic.

9 It's important to make sure the grout is wet. This makes it dry out slowly and prevents it from cracking. You can also cover the work with a warm, wet rag to slow down the drying process.

- **Note:** apply the grout at least one day after finishing the gluing, so as to make sure the mosaic doesn't fall apart.
- **Important:** do not stop in the middle of the grouting process. Make time and do this part well, from beginning to end, for the optimal result.

Project: Butterflies Pot Plant

I don't know anyone who doesn't like butterflies! You can see them in so many colors and shapes, and when looking closer, you can only marvel at their gentleness and magical creation.

Butterflies pot plants fit every garden, you can make them in any color scale you'd like, and if you're making it out of glass – it will also shine in the sunlight.

Since the pot plant is round and can be seen from several directions, I chose to decorate it with two different butterflies, each with a different shade and shape.

Materials:

- A 30 cm ceramics pot plant, or any other size you've like
- Glass in shades of blue, light blue, white, two shades of red, gray and black
- Golden circles
- Colorful Millefiori circles
- Glass squares in shades of light blue
- A big, circle for the butterfly's head

- A glass cutter
- Wooden stick or spatula to apply the glue
- A thin screwdriver or toothpick to clean the excess glue
- Tile glue
- Small bowl for the glue
- Cream-colored grout
- Grout equipment: Bowl, water, mixing stick, spatula, rags, paper, and gloves.

1 Using tracing paper and a pencil, copy the butterflies' patterns onto the pot – one on each side.

2 Cut light blue, blue, and black or gray glass into little pieces.

3 Trace the shape of the center of the butterfly onto black glass using a permanent marker. Cut out the whole shape using a glass cutter, and glue it in the middle for the butterfly (see glass cutting explanations on page 37).

4 Add blue glass around the center of the butterfly, and the cut-up gray glass as a contour around it.

5 Fill in the wings of the butterfly with blue glass cut up in different sizes.

6 Add antennas made out of Millefiori circles.

7 Second butterfly: Glue the center in the same way as the first one. Add a line of golden circles in the center of the wings.

8 Cut-up black glass into thin strips that will be used as separating lines inside the butterfly wings.

9 Glue the glass strips and place between them thin, cut-up rectangles from red glass.

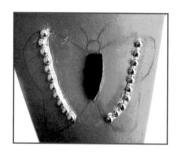

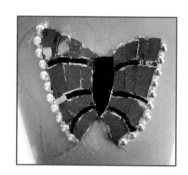

10 Cut up squares from the second shade of red glass, then cut each rectangle into thin strips.

11 Fill out the external part of the butterfly with red horizontal strips, add a yellow circle for the head and Millefiori circles for the antennas.

12 Cut up white glass into small pieces and fill in the background of the pot, between the butterflies. You can also incorporate Millefiori circles into the background.

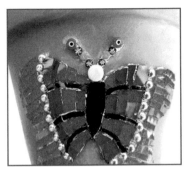

13 Prepare grout according to manufacturer's instructions, apply, and clean well.

Pattern for the butterflies:
Copy and enlarge according to the desire size.

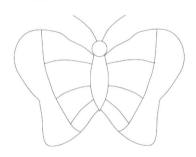

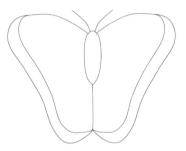

Project: Butterfly on Glass Plate

I received a set of blue, beautiful, glass plates that I no longer needed, but I felt were perfect for mosaics. I had to find the perfect pattern, and I think that white butterflies certainly fit the blue glass. I gathered all sorts of white materials – various pieces of glass and beads – and created the butterflies showing here.

In these examples, you can see two designs for the same pattern. You're welcome to look for a nice plate that would serve as a good setting as well as background, and create your butterfly according to the materials you find.

Materials:

- Blue glass plate
- White glass
- Various white beads
- Wheeled nipper
- A wooden stick to apply the glue

- A thin screwdriver to clean the excess glue
- Glass glue
- Small bowl for the glue
- Light-gray grout (optional)

1 Print out the butterfly pattern in the desired size and copy it onto the glass plate using a crayon (see explanations in previous projects).

2 Cut out glass into thin strips and glue onto the plate with beads, using glass glue/transparent silicon glue (you should use gloves). Create the butterfly's antennas from beads, and the butterfly's body from one part or three large parts.

3 Complete the butterfly this way, make sure to keep it clean. Remove any excess glue using a toothpick and a moist wipe or wet rag.

4 If you'd like, mix light-gray grout and apply on the butterfly itself. If you glued the pieces close together or used special beads, you can skip the grout. Glue it on the wall using strong silicone glue so the plate doesn't slide down; reinforce with two nails that you can remove a few hours later.

Pattern for the butterfly:
Copy and enlarge according to the desire size.

Cutting Glass into Strips

We cut the glass using a technique used in the art of stained glass by scoring the glass with a blade, then separating the two pieces.

To achieve maximum accuracy, each piece is machine-sanded after cutting. In this book, we'll only be using the blade and nipper.

There are several types of blades and hand grips. It's recommended that you use a quality cutter to make prolonged work more comfortable.

In order to cut accurate glass strips, use the cutting blade, L-square and pliers. First, we'll learn how to use the cutter.

For this purpose, you will need: a good glass knife, wooden L-square and a Breaking glass plier.

Steps of glass cutting - straight line:
* It is recommended to practice on clear and simple glass.

1. Place the panel you want to cut on a clean, level surface.
2. In order to cut a straight, accurate line, use a framing square or T-square: Place the square on the line you wish to cut.

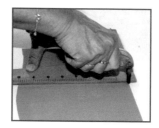

3. Hold the glass cutter with your dominant hand and dip it in oil if necessary (required with certain types of cutters).
4. Place the cutter at the top or bottom edge of the glass and hold it straight, perpendicular to the glass.

5. Score the glass lengthwise with your dominant hand, while pressing on the square with your other hand to keep it in place. You can cut either from top to bottom or vice-versa. It's essential to do this while maintaining even pressure from edge to edge, otherwise the cut might become crooked. If you hear a slight ripping sound, you're doing it right.

6. Grab the glass by its bottom with running plier and snap it off. Note that the markings in the pliers are facing upward. The glass will snap in two along the line.

Cutting Glass into Strips by Size

1. Place the glass you wish to cut on a clean, level surface.
2. Using a glass marker and T square, mark the width you want to cut. You can mark all the desired lines in advance.
3. Place the T-square on the glass. Begin cutting the strips in order as explained before. Leave the wide part of the glass for last. Repeat stages 3-6 of glass cutting.

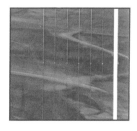

Cutting Glass into Shapes and Using the Pliers

Cutting glass into shapes is a somewhat complex action. Because of this, some shapes take several steps to cut and it's advised that you first practice on plain, clear glass. We'll use a glass knife, a running plier and a breaking plier. A running plier is a special two-sided plier, with one side being straight, and the other curved. The straight side is intended for separating between the two parts of the glass that were scored, and the curved side is for cutting – removing small pieces in the created shape in order to improve it, as a wheeled nipper sometimes does.

How to cut the glass:

1. Draw the shape you want to cut out on the glass using a permanent marker.
2. Leave space around, and don't draw the shape too close to the edge, so that it will be easier to separate the parts.
3. Cut the shape gradually in order to make cutting easier (see image). After making the groove, hold the cut-out shape with one hand, hold the pliers with its straight part upwards in the other, and perform a downward motion to cut out the excess part.
4. You can keep marking additional cuts after the initial one, and cut out the shape gradually, until the entire shape is completed.
5. To finalize it, you can put it through a sanding machine or refine it using a wheeled nipper, or the curved part of the breaking pliers.
6. You should hold on to the leftovers, you'll always find use for them.

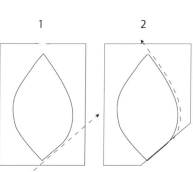

Project: Hanging Owls

The owl is one of my, and many other people's, favorite animal. I found owls made out of thick, strong Styrofoam in the hobby shop, and decided to coat them with mosaic and use a string to hang them on the tree branches in my yard. The owls are covered with colorful glass and mirror strips that make them glisten beautifully in the sunlight.

The Styrofoam goes through a coating process that makes it durable. It's also not a heavy material, the glass added to it isn't too heavy, and it can be easily hung. Other than the glass, you can incorporate beads, buttons, mirrors, glass circles, and other various materials. Every side can be different, as you'll see in the following examples.

You can make this owl from any basis you find, and you can also cut it out of a thick Styrofoam surface that you can find.

Materials:

- Styrofoam owl
- Glass cutting equipment
- A wooden stick or spatula to apply the glue
- A thin screwdriver or toothpick to clean the excess glue
- Tile glue
- Small bowl for the glue
- Cream-colored grout
- Strong, transparent fishing wire
- Grout equipment: Bowl, water, mixing stick, spatula, rags, paper, and gloves.

Pattern for the owl:
Copy and enlarge according to the desire size.

1 Cut out the owl shape in Styrofoam and make a hole to hang it at the top part, using a screwdriver or a wooden toothpick.

2 Coat the owl on all sides with tile glue. Smooth it out as much as possible using a little bit of water, and let it dry. It's recommended to leave the toothpick in, to keep the hanging hole open.

3 Draw the pattern of the owl and its details using a marker.

4 Start from the eyes – using tile glue, glue on nuggets or black buttons for the center of the eyes, and trapezoid-shaped cut glass around them.

5 Add a nose using glass cut up as a rhombus; complete the ears and fill in the face of the owl with glass cut up into small pieces.

6 Glue on the wings – in this sample, I used ready-made shapes, cut into random shapes.

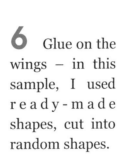

7 The belly – here you can combine different materials in addition to the cut-up glass, in this image: a large button.

8 After one side has dried out, glue the other side the same way (and you can combine other materials and colors).

9 In order to coat the glass strips, cut out strips of mirrors to the size of the side of the owl, then cut each strip into half.

10 Glue the glass strips close together on the owl's circumference.

11 Wait a day for it to dry and make grout, according to the manufacturer's instructions, for both sides of the owl and its circumference. It's important to keep the hanging hole from closing; hang the owl using a strong and transparent fishing line.

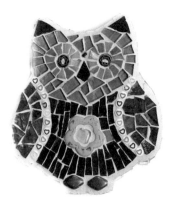

Project: Bird on a Wooden Flower Box

The hummingbird is one of my favorite birds. Little, quick, colorful, and beautiful birds with long beaks for sucking out nectar.

In this project, I coated a wooden flower box with glass mosaic of a bird and flowers. The glass has wonderful shades that accentuate the bird's body. The bird is made out of pieces that resemble thin strips in various shades that create motion.

Note: this wooden flower box can only be placed in a dry and humid-free place, since wood tends to swell up in wet, humid conditions, and the mosaic might fall off.cut it out of a thick Styrofoam surface that you can find.

Materials:

- A wooden flower box (or a rectangle wooden board for the image)
- Glass in shades of light blue, purple, black, green, yellow and white
- Glass circles – nuggets
- A small, black circle for the eye
- Wheeled nipper
- Ceramics cutting nipper
- Strong, white adhesive
- Pencil
- Paintbrush
- Small bowl for glue
- Gray grout
- Grout equipment: Bowl, water, mixing stick, spatula, rags, paper, and gloves.

1 Prepare the work surface – a wooden flower box or board, a bit rugged and without any lacquer.

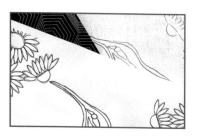

2 Using tracing paper and pencil, copy the patterns onto the work surface.

3 Using the wheeled nipper, cut out black glass into thin strips. Glue them on the edge of the beak and slightly under it. Glue a black eye for the bird.

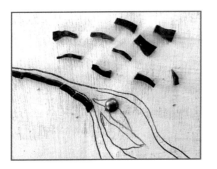

4 Cut thin strips in shades of light blue, light green, blue, and purple the same way.

5 Glue the light blue and green pieces closely together at the top part of the head, and the darker pieces at the bottom part.

6 Create the tail and body of the bird from light blue strips, dark purple for the outline and light green at the top part of the wing.

7 The wing of the bird is made out of strips in alternating light and dark purple.

8 Glue glass circles or ellipses at the center of each flower.

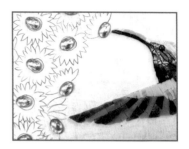

9 Cut out the flower petals: first, cut a rectangle out of yellow glass. Then, cut thin strips diagonally, so you get uneven triangles and rhombuses. It's better to cut out several shades of yellow or used versatile glass.

10 Glue the petals closely around the glass circles, each flower separately.

11 Cutting the leaves: cut out a long, thin glass rectangle. Then, cut out wide rhombuses using the wheeled nipper.

12 Round the edges of the rhombus to get the shape of a leaf. You can do that using the wheeled nipper or ceramic cutting nippers by holding it the other way and gently nibbling until the sharp edge is curved.

13 Make a lot of leaves that way.

14 Glue the leaves closely around the flower clusters.

15 To make the background, cut out white glass into various shapes and fill it in. It's important to keep the edges straight, to make it look aesthetic.

16 Wait a day for drying, prepare grout according to the manufacturer's instructions; apply and shine.

Pattern for the bird:
Copy and enlarge according to the desire size.

Project: Lace Mandala with a Butterfly

Mandalas hold a special charm. They're calming, focusing and allow flow… here I chose to combine a mandala with a butterfly, which is also a symmetrical creature, and it all comes together in a harmony of calming colors – white, pink, and purple. The pattern was inspired by lace, that has a gentle and circular pattern. The glass adds shades, creating depth and combining precisely-cut shapes by a cut-out traced onto the glass, and other cuts – triangles, rectangles, and random shapes.

Materials:

- A round wooden surface 11"/28 cm in diameter
- Glass in white, pink and purple shades
- 1X1 cm glass squares
- Little glass circles
- Tracing paper
- Pencil
- Glass-tracing marker

- White, strong glue
- Paintbrush
- Wheeled nipper
- Glass cutting equipment
- Small bowl for the glue
- Light gray grout
- Grout equipment: Bowl, water, mixing stick, spatula, rags, paper, and gloves.

1 Copy the pattern onto the wooden surface using tracing paper.

2 Creating the butterfly: cut out its parts out of paper. To create its bottom part, use a permanent marker to mark each part separately on pink glass, also mark Left and Right.

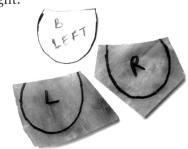

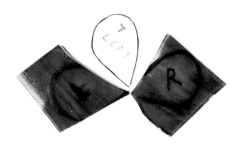

3 Mark the top part of the butterfly in the same way on purple glass.

4 Using a glass cutting knife, cut out the butterfly parts, sand it with a wheeled nipper or glass sander, and glue in place. Add beads to fit the body.

5 Glue little, pink, randomly cut pieces of mosaic around the purple glass.

6 Glue little, purple, randomly cut pieces of mosaic around the pink glass.

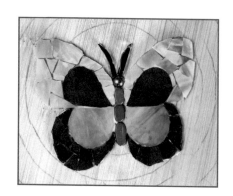

7 Cut out purple glass squares into rectangles and glue in a circle around the butterfly.

8 Cut white glass into thin strips and glue in a circle in their designated place.

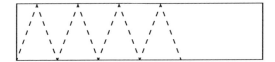

9 Cut up a long, narrow, purple glass rectangle, make triangles out of it, according to the above pattern.

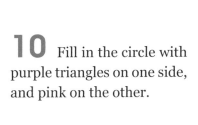

10 Fill in the circle with purple triangles on one side, and pink on the other.

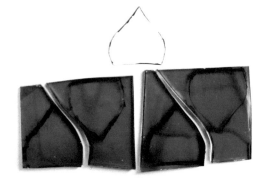

11 Cut up the leaves around the mandala in the same way you cut out the body of the butterfly – cut out one leaf, copy onto a purple glass, and cut up each leaf individually.

12 Glue the purple leaves around the mandala, in their right places.

13 Cut up thin, long, purple glass rectangles and create thin strips. Glue them on the outer part of the flower.

14 Similarly, cut out thin, pink glass strips and fill in the inner part of each leaf. Glue small, purple circles between the leaves.

15 Cut up white glass into random pieces and fill in the mandala's background.

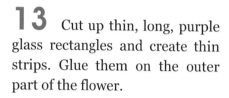

16 In case the round surface is thick, glue on purple glass squares around it, to form a contour.

17 Wait a day for it to dry. Prepare light grout according to the manufacturer's instructions. Apply it, clean and shine.

Pattern for the Mandala:
Copy and enlarge according to the desire size.

Project: Butterfly on a Net

When you want to hang mosaic on an exterior wall, a mesh might do the trick. You can make the following butterfly in many colors. What makes it special is its black contour, accentuating the colors, as well as the glue with which you choose to work.

I usually apply temporary glue on the mesh – carpenters' glue or white glue. This time, I chose to glue the glass onto the mesh using tile glue, so I can fill in the grout on the table and not on the wall, and then glue the complete work onto the wall.

This is a convenient and practical method that's great for small projects.

Materials:

- A flexible fiberglass mesh, cut into a desired-sized rectangle
- Cut up nylon, slightly bigger than the next
- Stapler
- Glass in a variety of shades of purple, yellow, orange, blue, red, light blue, and black
- Beads for the antennas
- Wheeled nipper for cutting glass
- Spatula or wooden stick
- Scissors
- Tile glue
- A little spatula to apply the glue
- A little screwdriver or toothpick to clean out the excess glue
- Cream-colored grout
- Grout equipment: Bowl, water, mixing stick, spatula, rags, paper, and gloves.

1 Print out the butterfly pattern; cut up a mesh and nylon to the right size. Use a stapler to attach the three pieces in the following order: butterfly, above it nylon and eventually the mesh.

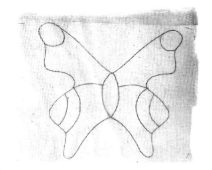

2 Cut thin strips out of black glass, the width of the strips has to do with the thickness of the contour you'd like to make (see explanation for cutting glass into strips on page 36).

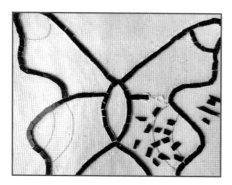

3 Cut up the black glass strips into little rectangles and trapezoids and glue them along the butterfly's outline using tile glue. Clean off the excess glue using the screwdriver or toothpick. You should use a spatula or a piping bag.

4 Fill in the butterfly's body: cut yellow glass into small, random pieces, and fill in the center of the butterfly; and pink/purple glass for its bottom part.

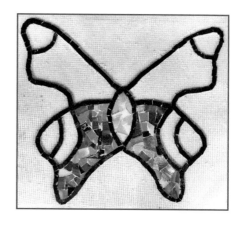

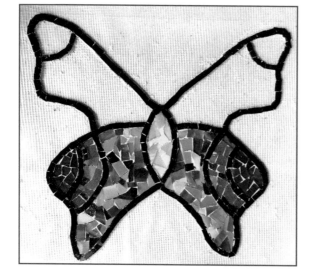

5 Cut up orange-shaded glass into little pieces and fill in, as shown.

6 The top of the butterfly is made out of little red and light blue pieces of glass.

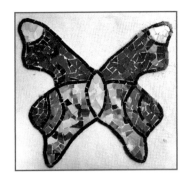

7 Wait a day or two for it to dry out, separate the mesh from the nylon and cut as close to the mesh as possible. Apply light-colored grout as per the manufacturer's instructions; clean and shine.

8 A few hours later, when the grout is dry, gently flip the butterfly upside down (you should use a wooden board or thick cardboard). Peel off the nylon, apply tile glue on the back, and stick it to the wall. Glue the bead-made antennas directly onto the wall.

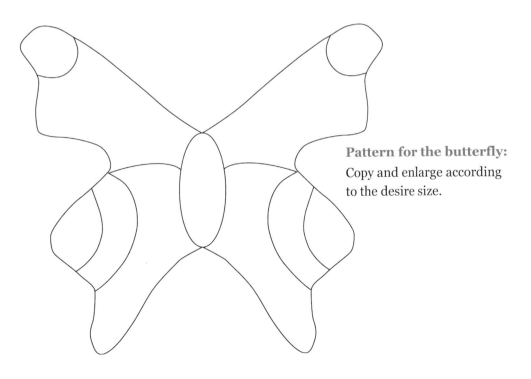

Pattern for the butterfly:
Copy and enlarge according to the desire size.

Project: A Picture of a Cat with Butterflies

If you love animals, as I do, you'd certainly agree that a cat looking at butterflies is a nice image. The question is, is it looking at them fly or working out how to catch one of them? We'll leave that for your imagination.

This picture is made out of glass mosaic, so you can get an abundance of colors and combine many shades. Additionally, it combines different types of cuts – thin strips for the cat, random cuts for the background, and whole, well-defined pieces for the butterflies.

There are two types of butterflies in the air, one in shades of blue, and the other in shades of yellow. A brown-shaded cat looks at them with green-shaded foliage around it. The background is made out of shades of white and pink that get darker at it advances upwards.

A real, colorful celebration!

Materials:

- A 40X40 cm wooden board
- Glass in various shades of red, yellow, blue, light blue, black, green, brown, pink, and white
- Glass cutting nipper
- Glass cutting knife
- White glue
- Small bowl for glue
- Paintbrush to apply the glue
- Tweezers
- A moist towelette to clean the excess glue
- Light gray grout
- Grout equipment: a bowl, water, mixing stick, spatula, rags, newspapers, and gloves.

1 Print out the pattern to the desired size and trace it onto the wooden board. Go over it with a marker, if necessary.

2 Yellow butterfly: cut up a glass strip the width of the butterfly's body, then into rectangles and trapezoid. Fit them together from the narrow part to the wide one, and back to the narrow one. Glue on a black circle for the butterfly's head.

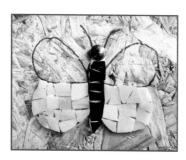

3 Cut up yellow glass into squares and trapezoids and glue at the bottom part of the butterfly.

4 Similarly, cut darker shaded glass (with a hue of orange) and glue at the top of the butterfly. Add antennas from the orange glass. Glue the rest of the yellow butterflies the same way.

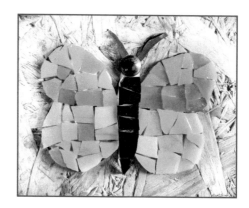

5 Blue butterfly: glue on the butterfly's black body, as you did with the yellow ones. Cut up red glass circles and glue them at their place on each wing.

6 The bottom part of the butterfly: glue on light-blue glass at the inner part of the circle, and blue glass at the outer part of it.

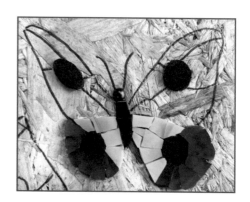

7 Glue two shades of green glass on the top part of the wings.

8 The cat: cut up black glass, and glue it on a rounded-edge triangle for the nose, a thin strip for the mouth, and another one for the center of the eye. Glue on two green triangles around it to complete the eye.

9 The cat's tail is made out of black rectangles that are glued closely together. Cut out half ellipses and glue them on as the paws.

10 Glue on a pink triangle to the center of the front ear, with brown pieces around it. Glue on a brown triangle for the other ear. Cut up glass in various light-brown shades and fill in the cat's face. Add darker tones where needed, at the bottom of the neck.

11 Keep gluing on pieces this way throughout the cat's body. You can also mix in shades according to the glass you have. You should differentiate between the legs by using different shades of glass.

12 Cut up dark-green glass into random pieces and glue them under the cat's body.

13 Keep adding different shades of green areas the same way, until you complete the bottom part of the picture.

14 Cut up white and pink glass into random pieces and create the background – white pieces at the bottom, pink at the top, and a combination of the two in the middle, to create a gradual transition.

15 Prepare gray grout according to the manufacturer's instructions; apply and fill in all the cracks. Clean with a damp rag until the mosaic is clean. Shine with a moist towelette, add a strong hanging point in the back, and enjoy your new creation!

Tip: When gluing on the butterflies, instead of gluing on each butterfly from start to finish and then moving on to the next one, you should work laterally: first glue on all the butterflies' bodies, then all of the yellow glass, then all the orange, and so on.

Pattern for the Picture:
Copy and enlarge according to the desire size.

Project: Water Birds

Some birds can be found in the sky, but I'd also like to cherish the beautiful water birds.

This project is a bit complex, both in terms of its size (40X60 cm) and for its combination of materials: glass, beads, stones, a plate, mirrors and seashells. Since it's a picture, you don't have to maintain a clean look, on the contrary, there's a beauty to combining materials of different textures and thicknesses, each of them adding character to the work, giving it another dimension.

Each material has its own texture: the water birds are made out of a broken plate, glass, and shiny mirrors.

The island in the center of the lake is made out of small, colorful glass stones.

The mountains: made out of brown-shaded glass and glass beads.

At the bottom of the picture: special seashells I had collected at the beach.

Once the picture was glued onto the wall, it seemed to be missing something, so I added another part – you can see it later on and obviously find both patterns in the patterns file.

Materials:

- A flexible fiberglass mesh cut out to a 40X60 cm rectangle
- Nylon, cut out slightly bigger than the mesh
- Stapler
- Glass in various shades of light blue, white, green, brown, red, orange, yellow, black, and blue
- Brown beads
- Eye-shaped beads
- Mirrors
- Seashells
- Little stones
- A green plate
- Wheeled nipper for cutting glass
- Paintbrush
- Scissors
- Carpenter's glue or white glue
- Light and dark-gray grout
- Grout equipment: a bowl, water, mixing stick, spatula, rags, newspapers and gloves

1 Print out the picture pattern (you can print it in sections with a home printer and then attach them, or print it out at a copy shop in the original size). Cut out the mesh and nylon at the right sizes. Use a stapler to attach the three parts in the following order: paper, above it nylon, and finally the mesh.

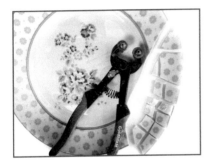

2 PWater birds: choose a plate with the right texture and cut it up, using a wheeled nipper, into small pieces to fit the birds' wings (see explanation on cutting cups and plates).

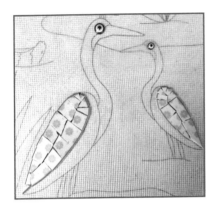

3 Glue the cut-up parts onto the birds' wings. Add an eye to fit each of the birds.

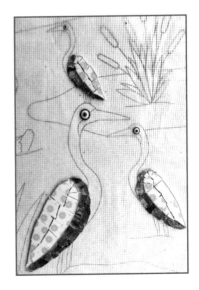

4 Cut up red glass into small pieces and complete the birds' bodies.

5 Cut up mirrors to create the birds' necks. Make the beak out of orange glass and the feet out of black glass.

6 Cut up orange, blue, and green glass and glue them on the duck, as shown. Add an eye and a beak cut out of two orange glass parts.

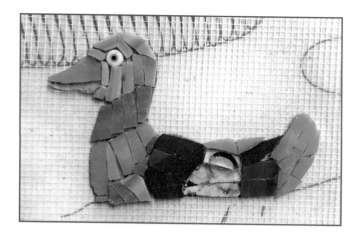

7 Cattail plant: to create the flowers, cut up yellow glass to thin rectangles. Round off the edges of the rectangle using a wheeled nipper or ceramics nipper held in the opposite direction.

8 Cut up two shades of green glass into strips and glue them in the right place, to create the leaves and stalks.

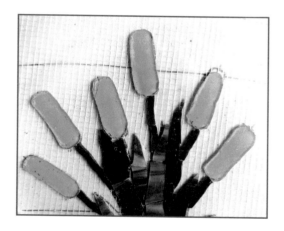

9 The island is made out of small glass stones: apply a relatively large amount of glue on the mesh, sprinkle stones on it, and press down.

10 The vegetation above the duck is made out of a green plate cut up into thin strips. You can also create it from green cup.

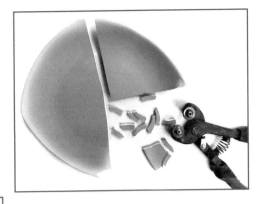

11 Glue on the green strips as closely as possible.

12 The big plant: cut up green glass into long rectangles, then each rectangle into smaller pieces.

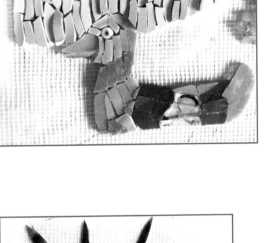

13 Glue on each leaf individually, closely together, with a pointy triangle at their top. It's recommended to use two shades of green to create some separation between the leaves.

14 The mountains: cut up various shades of brown glass into random pieces and glue a different color onto each strip. You can add a strip of brown beads.

15 The background is made out of light-blue glass strips, and a little bit of green cut out of glass squares in the following manner: hold the square diagonally, with the pointy tip facing up. Cut a triangle at the tip and keep cutting vertical thin strips. You will get elongated shapes, sometimes pointy ones, not always even ones, but that is all right – since the wheels of the nipper don't always cut in a straight line.

16 Similarly, cut up a few strips from white rectangles and glue them on for the waves, then fill in the entire background.

17 Glue on pieces of large, versatile, black glass at the bottom of the picture.

18 Wait a day or two for it to dry, separate the mesh from the nylon, and cut as close to the mosaic as possible.

19 Using a spatula or putty knife, apply tile glue on the back of the picture. The amount of glue should be enough to cover the mesh but don't apply too thinly.

20 Attach the mosaic picture to the wall and tighten. You can gently hit it with your hands or a wooden hammer to completely stick all the pieces. Take out whatever viable glue is left using a thin screwdriver before it all dries up.

21 Wait for it to dry at least 24 hours, and finish it off with grout, directly on the wall. You can use dark grout for the darker parts and light grout for the rest. Start with the dark grout, clean, and wait a bit for it to dry; then fill in the light grout and clean.

22 **Important**: In case you've used small stones to fill out an area, you shouldn't put grout on them, rather leave them as they are – glue only.

23 If you'd like to add seashells, as I did, glue them on after the grout process is completed, directly onto the wall, using a strong silicone glue.

On the top right is the continuation picture of the water birds (the drawing can be found in the patterns file).

Pattern for the birds picture:
Copy and enlarge according to the desire size.

Cutting Mugs and Cups using a Wheeled Nipper

1   Hold the nipper with your dominant hand, and support the piece with your other hand. Bring the nipper to the rim, with the wheels clutching it from both sides.

2   Firmly press the nipper until the piece is cut.

3   Keep cutting the parts of the mug using the nipper.

4   Remove excess parts and reduce them to the desired size.

Cutting a plate using a wheeled nipper

1 Hold on to the nipper with your dominant hand and the plate with the other.

2 Put the nipper closer to the center of the plate, with the wheels clutching it on both sides, and click. The wheels will cut the plate.

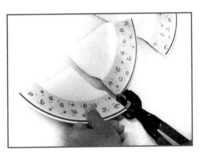

3 Keep cutting the plate to quarters in the same way, then to smaller pieces.

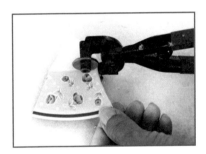

4 When the parts are smaller, you can easily take off the excess by cutting them again.

Project: Three-Dimensional Bird

This bird is 3D, meaning it has volume, and some pieces are glued one on top of the other, covered with glass mosaic on all sides.

You can make the bird out of Styrofoam or use other materials such as Wedi board, which can be bought in stores that specialize in building materials. This material can be cut with a knife, is resistant to weather, and can be glued on an exterior wall.

The bird is covered with various shades of glass; I've added a branch and leaves, also cut from the same material.

Here I used dark-gray colored glue, so I could also make the grout in the same color.

Materials:

- A thick (at least 2 cm) Styrofoam board or wedi board
- Glass or glass squares in various shades of blue, red, orange, black, white, green, and brown
- Wheeled nipper for cutting glass
- Tile glue
- A small bowl for the glue
- A wooden stick or spatula for applying glue
- A box cutter

- A thin screwdriver or toothpick to clean excess glue
- Marker
- A glass-cutting knife
- Black acrylic paint
- Piping bag
- Dark-gray grout
- Grout equipment: a bowl, water, mixing stick, spatula, rags, newspapers and gloves

1 Print out the bird pattern, cut and trace onto the Styrofoam board, including the branch.

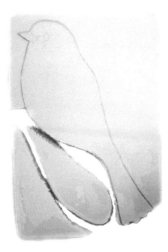

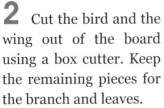

2 Cut the bird and the wing out of the board using a box cutter. Keep the remaining pieces for the branch and leaves.

3 Using a box cutter, "sand off" the edges of the wing to make it rounder and take off any sharp edges.

4 Clean any leftover material around the wing and the bird, and smooth them out as much as possible.

5 Put on gloves and glue the wing of the bird in place using tile glue. Keep coating the bird on the front and the sides; use water to smooth it out, when necessary.

6 Cut out blue and light-blue glass squares into thin strips to create the wing.

7 In a bowl, mix tile glue and a little black acrylic paint to create a gray color.

Tip: You should make enough glue to last right up to the end of the project. This is why you should use a piping bag, make a lot of colored glue and put it into the bag. Close the bag using a clip and keep it in a closed box.

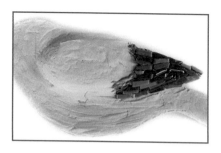

8 Complete gluing the wing, combine lighter shades, including the rounded edges.

9 The bird's wing: Glue dark-blue strips on the narrow part of the wing.

10 Add a black circle for an eye, and form the beak out of black glass.

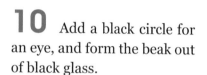

11 Cut up colorful glass into thin strips and glue on the bird's body: very light blue for the head; brown, yellow, red, and orange for the belly; and then once again light colors, just before the tail.

12 The bird's tail: Strips of light blue and silver or mirror, to accentuate the strips.

13 Cut up black glass into strips (or use ready-made squares) and coat the bird on all sides.

14 Wait a day for it to dry and prepa[re] gray grout, according to the manufacture[r] instructions. Apply on the bird, then clea[n] and shine.

15 Cut out two branch pieces and a few leaves from the leftover Styrofoam. Coat with tile glue, the same way as before, and glue on green and brown glass. If possible, cut out complete pieces for the leaves.

16 Glue black glass on the parameter of these pieces as well, and finish with gray grout.

17 Glue the bird onto the wall using tile glue or strong silicone glue. Add the branch and leaves where you'd like them.

Pattern for the bird:
Copy and enlarge according to the desire size.

Additional Bird Patterns

Birds glued on wood, cut to size.

Glass, glass squares, molding clay, and beads.

Smalti, glass, and beads.

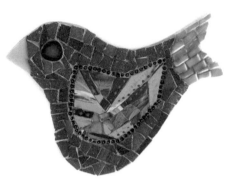

Painted glass, glass squares, and beads.

Ready-made shapes, mirrors, and beads.

Glass, cut-up plates and cups, and beads

Canvas pictures that combine mosaic with acrylic paint

Various beads and ready-made shapes, pasted on
black painted canvas

Glass, glass circles, and beads

Glass, glass circles, shredded glass,
and beads

Pictures

Glass and glass squares

Glass and beads on a metal background,
with a wooden frame

Glass, cut-up cups and plates, and beads

Natural stone squares and colorful marble

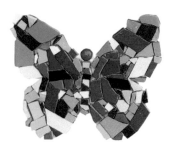

Summary

In this book – the tenth of the Mosaic for Beginners series – I've chosen to show patterns that have to do with birds and butterflies. The possibilities are so vast and the nature around us is so rich, providing so much inspiration.

You can use the ideas in this book as you'd like: mixing materials, changing colors to match your preferences, or creating something new based on what you've seen.

This book showed projects that might suit exterior walls as well as indoors. We talked about various bases and beds on which to glue the mosaic: pot plants, wooden board pictures, meshs, Styrofoam, as well as recycled kitchenware.

This book has shown various cutting techniques and differentiated between cutting glass and ceramics. Each of them uses different tools as well as slightly different cutting techniques.

The birds and butterflies in this book are made using various techniques and materials, and there are a multitude of examples for combining materials: ceramics, glass, mirrors, beads, stones, seashells, plates, and cups – all to show that anything is possible in mosaic!

In my studio, the students prepared these butterflies on a mesh as part of a large national commemoration project honoring the October 2023 martyrs.

It's important to be creative; you can use materials you have around the house or look for ones that would fit the specific project you'd like to make. The current selection of materials available for mosaics is immense, and you should explore the different combinations.

This book has shown some examples to create birds and butterflies, but mosaic work is quite endless; it's important to learn the basics and then let your imagination soar, making up your own patterns or looking for inspiration in different places.

I hope I was able to convey some of my love for the world of mosaic through this book. Take the ideas you liked from this book and create your own birds and butterflies. Don't hesitate to combine materials, try and see which materials you like and what aspect of mosaics best suits you.Keep it creative,

Keep your creativity alive,

Yours,

Sigalit Eshet

Other mosaic books on Amazon:

Amazing Mosaic Garden:
Surprising Designs in
Various Techniques

Mosaic Hamsas: Original
Designs and Various
Techniques

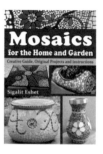

Mosaics for the
Home and Garden

The Magic Mesh:
Mosaic Mesh Projects

Stained Glass Mosaic

Beautiful Mosaic Flowers

Mosaic Glass Pictures

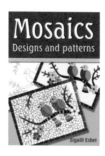

Mosaics - Designs
and patterns

Mosaics: Great Ideas
and Projects

There is a bonus for you. All the patterns that are showed in this book, are available in a pdf file, for your use:

Just type **https://bit.ly/3R5VssP** in your browser and get it or scan the QR.

If from some reason you can't get the file, please email me and I will mail it to you: **sigalit@sigalit.art**

If you loved this book, **Please leave a review on Amazon** and let other people enjoy making a great mosaic garden.

✉ **Sigalit@sigalit.art**

🌐 **www.sigalit.art**

f **SigalitBooks**

etsy **Sigalitarts**

a **amazon.com/author/sigaliteshet**

Made in the USA
Columbia, SC
03 April 2024

33927304R00049